Antonio VIVALDI

(1678 – 1741)

Sonata for Cello and Basso continuo (Piano)
Op. 14 No. 3, RV 43
A minor / la mineur / a-moll

Edited by
Josef Hofer

DOWANI International

Preface

This edition presents a piece that belongs in the standard repertoire of every cellist: the Sonata for cello and basso continuo Op. 14 No. 3, RV 43 in A minor by Antonio Vivaldi. It allows you to work through the piece systematically and at different tempi with a piano accompaniment.

The CD begins with the concert version of each movement. After tuning your instrument (Track 1), the musical work can begin. First, you will hear the piano accompaniment at slow tempo for practice purposes; you can also hear the cello played softly in the background as a guide. You can also practice the second movement at medium tempo (piano accompaniment only). We decided against presenting a medium tempo for movements 1 and 3 since they are already relatively slow. Having mastered these levels, you can now play with a piano accompaniment at the original tempo. All of the versions were recorded live. The names of the musicians are listed on the last page of this volume; further information can be found in the Internet at www.dowani.com.

The fingering and bowing marks in this edition were provided by Josef Hofer, a cellist and teacher living in Liechtenstein. Hofer studied with Walter Grimmer in Berne and Gerhard Mantel in Frankfurt am Main. He is well known as a chamber musician and jury member at various national and international competitions and has taught for many years in Liechtenstein and Switzerland.

We wish you lots of fun playing from our *DOWANI 3 Tempi Play Along* editions and hope that your musicality and diligence will enable you to play the concert version as soon as possible.

It is our goal to give you the essential conditions for effective practicing through motivation, enjoyment and fun.

Your DOWANI Team

Avant-propos

Cette édition vous présente un morceau qui fait partie du répertoire standard de tous les violoncellistes : la sonate pour violoncelle et basse continue op. 14 n° 3, RV 43 en la mineur d'Antonio Vivaldi. Cette édition vous offre la possibilité de travailler l'œuvre d'une manière systématique dans différents tempos avec accompagnement de piano.

Le CD vous permettra d'entendre d'abord la version de concert de chaque mouvement. Après avoir accordé votre instrument (plage N° 1), vous pourrez commencer le travail musical. Pour travailler le morceau au tempo lent, vous entendrez l'accompagnement de piano ; le violoncelle restera cependant toujours audible très doucement à l'arrière-plan. Vous pourrez également travailler le 2ème mouvement à un tempo modéré (seulement avec l'accompagnement de piano). Les 1er et 3ème mouvements ne sont pas proposés dans un tempo modéré, car leurs tempos originaux sont déjà relativement lents. Vous pourrez ensuite jouer le tempo original avec accompagnement de piano. Toutes les versions ont été enregistrées en direct. Vous trouverez les noms des artistes qui ont participé aux enregistrements sur la dernière page de cette édition ; pour obtenir plus de renseignements, veuillez consulter notre site Internet : www.dowani.com.

Les doigtés et indications des coups d'archet proviennent du violoncelliste et pédagogue Josef Hofer qui vit au Liechtenstein. Il étudia auprès de Walter Grimmer à Berne et Gerhard Mantel à Francfort-sur-le-Main. Josef Hofer est musicien de chambre et membre de jury de divers concours nationaux et internationaux.

Il enseigne depuis de nombreuses années au Liechtenstein et en Suisse.

Nous vous souhaitons beaucoup de plaisir à faire de la musique avec la collection *DOWANI 3 Tempi Play Along* et nous espérons que votre musicalité et votre application vous amèneront aussi rapidement que possible à la version de concert.

Notre but est de vous offrir les bases nécessaires pour un travail efficace par la motivation et le plaisir.

Les Éditions DOWANI

Vorwort

Mit dieser Ausgabe präsentieren wir Ihnen ein Stück, das zum Standardrepertoire eines jeden Cellisten zählt: die Sonate für Violoncello und Basso continuo op. 14 Nr. 3, RV 43 in a-moll von Antonio Vivaldi. Diese Ausgabe ermöglicht es Ihnen, das Werk systematisch und in verschiedenen Tempi mit Klavierbegleitung zu erarbeiten.

Auf der CD hören Sie zuerst die Konzertversion eines jeden Satzes. Nach dem Stimmen Ihres Instrumentes (Track 1) kann die musikalische Arbeit beginnen. Zum Üben folgt nun im langsamen Tempo die Klavierbegleitung, wobei das Cello als Orientierung leise im Hintergrund zu hören ist. Den 2. Satz können Sie auch im mittleren Tempo üben (nur Klavierbegleitung). Beim 1. und 3. Satz haben wir auf das mittlere Tempo verzichtet, da die Sätze schon relativ langsam sind. Anschließend können Sie sich im Originaltempo begleiten lassen. Alle eingespielten Versionen wurden live aufgenommen. Die Namen der Künstler fin-

den Sie auf der letzten Seite dieser Ausgabe; ausführlichere Informationen können Sie im Internet unter www.dowani.com nachlesen.

Die Fingersätze und Striche in dieser Ausgabe stammen von dem in Liechtenstein lebenden Cellisten und Pädagogen Josef Hofer. Er studierte bei Walter Grimmer in Bern sowie bei Gerhard Mantel in Frankfurt am Main. Josef Hofer ist als Kammermusiker und Jurymitglied bei diversen nationalen und internationalen Wettbewerben tätig und unterrichtet seit vielen Jahren in Liechtenstein und der Schweiz.

Wir wünschen Ihnen viel Spaß beim Musizieren aus *DOWANI 3 Tempi Play Along*-Ausgaben und hoffen, dass Ihre Musikalität und Ihr Fleiß Sie möglichst bald bis zur Konzertversion führen werden.

Unser Ziel ist es, Ihnen durch Motivation, Freude und Spaß die notwendigen Voraussetzungen für effektives Üben zu schaffen.

Ihr DOWANI Team

Sonata

for Cello and Basso continuo, Op. 14 No. 3, RV 43

A minor / la mineur / a-moll

A. Vivaldi (1678 – 1741)

Continuo Realization: G. Stöver

DOW 3502

Antonio VIVALDI

(1678 – 1741)

Sonata for Cello and Basso continuo (Piano)
Op. 14 No. 3, RV 43
A minor / la mineur / a-moll

Cello / Violoncelle / Violoncello

DOWANI International

Cello

Sonata

for Cello and Basso continuo, Op. 14 No. 3, RV 43
A minor / la mineur / a-moll

A. Vivaldi (1678 – 1741)
Edited by J. Hofer

DOW 3502

6

Antonio VIVALDI

(1678 – 1741)

Sonata for Cello and Basso continuo (Piano)
Op. 14 No. 3, RV 43
A minor / la mineur / a-moll

Basso continuo / Basse continue / Generalbass

DOWANI International

Sonata

for Cello and Basso continuo, Op. 14 No. 3, RV 43

A minor / la mineur / a-moll

A. Vivaldi (1678 – 1741)

I

II

DOW 3502

III

Largo

4

IV

Allegro

ENGLISH

DOWANI CD:
- Track No. 1

  | 1 | - tuning notes

- Track numbers in circles

  ⬤ - concert version

- Track numbers in squares

  ▭ (white/grey/black bar)

  - slow Play Along Tempo
  - intermediate Play Along Tempo
  - original Play Along Tempo

- Additional tracks for longer movements or pieces
- **Concert version:** cello and piano
- **Slow tempo:** piano accompaniment with cello in the background
- **Intermediate tempo:** piano accompaniment only
- **Original tempo:** piano accompaniment only

Please note that the recorded version of the piano accompaniment may differ slightly from the sheet music. This is due to the spontaneous character of live music making and the artistic freedom of the musicians. The original sheet music for the solo part is, of course, not affected.

FRANÇAIS

DOWANI CD:
- Plage N° 1

  | 1 | - diapason

- N° de plage dans un cercle

  ⬤ - version de concert

- N° de plage dans un rectangle

  ▭ (white/grey/black bar)

  - tempo lent play along
  - tempo moyen play along
  - tempo original play along

- Plages supplémentaires pour mouvements ou morceaux longs
- **Version de concert :** violoncelle et piano
- **Tempo lent :** accompagnement de piano avec violoncelle en fond sonore
- **Tempo moyen :** seulement l'accompagnement de piano
- **Tempo original :** seulement l'accompagnement de piano

L'enregistrement de l'accompagnement de piano peut présenter quelques différences mineures par rapport au texte de la partition. Ceci est du à la liberté artistique des musiciens et résulte d'un jeu spontané et vivant, mais n'affecte, bien entendu, d'aucune manière la partie soliste.

DEUTSCH

DOWANI CD:
- Track Nr. 1

  | 1 | - Stimmtöne

- Trackangabe im Kreis

  ⬤ - Konzertversion

- Trackangabe im Rechteck

  ▭ (white/grey/black bar)

  - langsames Play Along Tempo
  - mittleres Play Along Tempo
  - originales Play Along Tempo

- Zusätzliche Tracks bei längeren Sätzen oder Stücken
- **Konzertversion:** Violoncello und Klavier
- **Langsames Tempo:** Klavierbegleitung mit Violoncello im Hintergrund
- **Mittleres Tempo:** nur Klavierbegleitung
- **Originaltempo:** nur Klavierbegleitung

Die Klavierbegleitung auf der CD-Aufnahme kann gegenüber dem Notentext kleine Abweichungen aufweisen. Dies geht in der Regel auf die künstlerische Freiheit der Musiker und auf spontanes, lebendiges Musizieren zurück. Die Solostimme bleibt davon selbstverständlich unangetastet.

DOWANI - 3 Tempi Play Along is published by:
DOWANI International Est.
Industriestrasse 24 / Postfach 156, FL-9487 Bendern,
Principality of Liechtenstein
Phone: ++423 370 11 15, Fax ++423 370 19 44
Email: info@dowani.com
www.dowani.com

Recording & Digital Mastering: Pavel Lavrenenkov, Russia
CD-Production: Sonopress, Germany
Music Notation: Notensatz Thomas Metzinger, Germany
Design: Atelier Schuster, Austria
Printed by: Buchdruckerei Lustenau, Austria
Made in the Principality of Liechtenstein

Concert Version
Sergey Sudzilovsky, Cello
Vitaly Junitsky, Piano

3 Tempi Accompaniment
Slow:
Vitaly Junitsky, Piano

Intermediate:
Vitaly Junitsky, Piano

Original:
Vitaly Junitsky, Piano